CONTENTS

KU-739-662

Some words are shown in bold, **like this.** You can find out what they mean by looking in the glossary.

Visitors to the rainforests of Central America are fascinated by the ancient and dramatic buildings that tower above the dense jungle. These vast pyramids and temples are the remains of the complex civilization of the Maya, who flourished here for more than 2,000 years.

The first Maya settlers arrived in the lowland region of what is now central Mexico in around 800 BC. They came from the highlands further south in search of better farmland. After 600 BC, the early Maya villages grew into cities and in the centuries after 300 BC the Maya began to build great temples and pyramids in cities such as Tikal.

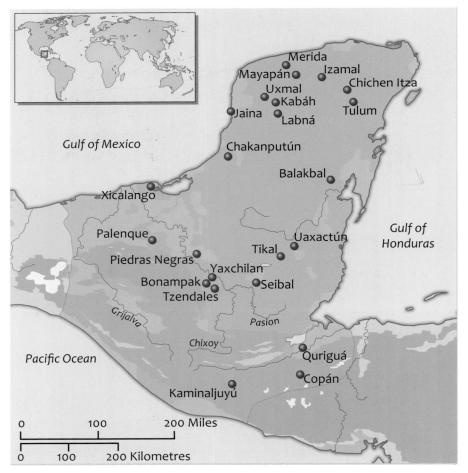

Maya **city-states** grew in the region that is now southern Mexico, Guatemala and Belize.

Maya civilization was at its most powerful during the Classic Period that began around AD 250, at the same time as much of Europe and North Africa was part of the Roman Empire.

The remains of Maya cities such as Palenque are still an awe-inspiring sight.

As well as their incredible buildings, the Maya developed a sophisticated system of writing and mathematics. Maya priests studied the movements of stars and planets and created a calendar that allows us to accurately date key events. However, **archaeologists** still have many mysteries to solve about this civilization, particularly about the daily life of ordinary people.

HOW DO WE KNOW?

In 1952, an international group of language experts unlocked the secrets of Maya writing. They discovered that some symbols represented sounds, while others showed a whole word or idea. Archaeologists used this information, together with knowledge of contemporary Maya people, to read the carvings and writings of the ancient Maya.

The Maya civilization was not a single country or an empire ruled from a central capital city. Archaeologists have uncovered more than 6,000 Maya settlements, including many large cities. The biggest Maya cities, such as Tikal, were home to as many as 100,000 people. During the Classic Period more than 40 Maya cities were home to 5,000 people or more. The Maya city-states were made up of cities and the farmland around them. Each had its own ruler.

In the city of El Mirador, the largest pyramid was as tall as a modern 18-storey building.

Centres of power

These cities were laid out very differently from modern towns. The heart of the city was where the king and the most powerful people in the city-state lived and worked. Palaces, temples and pyramids stood around grand squares, raised up above the surrounding city. This was where the city-state was governed from. Larger cities had more than one of these grand complexes, joined together by raised roads.

Temples were for public ceremonies, and usually had only one small room inside.

 EARLY THEORIES

Many of the grandest Maya cities were long abandoned by the time European explorers visited them, following the Spanish invasion of the area in the 1520s. These explorers didn't believe that the local people could have built the Maya monuments. They wrongly claimed that the cities had been built by everyone from the ancient Egyptians to Welsh settlers.

Living in the city

Alongside the temple-pyramids stood the palaces of the powerful. These were built on lower platforms than the temples. Their many rooms were set around courtyards and separated by ornate arches. Palaces grew over time as each ruler added new rooms. They were homes to the rulers but also used for governing the city and for royal celebrations, including feasting and dances.

Palaces and other public buildings were richly decorated with carvings and painted scenes.

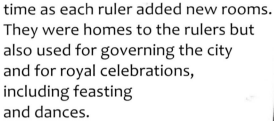

HOW DO WE KNOW?

One evening in AD 595, the Loma Caldera volcano erupted, burying the nearby village of Ceren in volcanic ash. The village was discovered by accident in 1978, perfectly preserved beneath the ash. The village has helped archaeologists understand much more about Mayan homes, food and daily life. The buildings of the village included houses, a feasting hall and a public bathhouse.

Beyond the city centre

Away from the palaces and pyramids stretched the part of the city where most people lived. Ordinary homes were often built on raised platforms to avoid flooding. These platforms have survived to show the layout of Maya cities.

Maya houses were not arranged along streets. The Maya had no wheeled vehicles or horses, so they had no need for roads. Instead, homes were arranged around small squares or courtyards. Homes were huts made of mud and sticks, with **thatched** roofs. Each courtyard group may have housed all members of a family.

Cities gradually spread out as the population grew and more homes were built. Unlike other ancient empires, Maya cities didn't usually have walls built around them for defence.

Feeding the city

The cities themselves were built on raised ground or ridges so they stood out above the surrounding farmland. The survival of the city depended on being able to grow food. If there wasn't enough water to grow crops, the harvest would fail and this could spell disaster.

Maya cities and farmland were created by clearing the thick rainforest that covered the land.

The landscape around the cities would have looked very different from the lush rainforests of today. The first farmers cleared the forest, removing the undergrowth with stone axes. This undergrowth was burned and the land could then be used to grow crops such as maize, the key ingredient of the Maya diet. Farmers gradually cleared more land as the Maya population grew. During the Classic Period of the Maya, this farmland would have stretched as far as the eye could see.

Precious water

Water was vital for growing crops, as well as for drinking, and the dry season could last for many months. Some city-states, such as Palenque, were close to rivers. Other had to find more inventive ways of preserving water. In Tikal, rainwater was collected on paved or plastered surfaces and directed through human-made channels and canals into a series of tanks and **reservoirs**.

 CENOTES

Many cities were built close to natural underground lakes called **cenotes**. At Bolonchen, Maya climbed down more than 100 metres (328 feet) to collect water. The city of Chichén Itzá was built close to two cenotes. One of these provided the city's water supply; the other was used for religious ceremonies and possibly human **sacrifices**.

This cenote was probably used for religious ceremonies and rituals.

Kings ruled Maya city-states, and they passed on power from one generation to the next. These kings were called "holy lords" and were the link between the Maya people and their gods. Kings appointed officials and generals, often members of their own families. They also commanded an army of servants.

The Maya city-states were independent of each other, though they shared the same culture and system of writing. Cities could be just a few kilometres apart, so the competition between them was fierce, and often deadly. A Maya king might have to lead his city-state in war against its rivals.

This king of Palenque is ready for war with his ornate headdress and spear.

King Pacal the Great

We know about King Pacal of Palenque from his dramatic tomb, which Mexican archaeologist Alberto Ruz discovered in 1952. Pacal ruled Palenque for an astonishing 68 years after becoming king in AD 615. He made Palenque into the most powerful state in the region, sealing **alliances** with other states such as Tikal.

Recording their rulers

We know a lot about the rulers of major Maya states such as Tikal and Palenque because their reigns were recorded in carvings on stone columns, known as **stelae**, and carved door **lintels**.

This funeral mask of King Pacal was made from shells and precious stones.

Lady of Tikal

Maya city-states were nearly always ruled by kings, rather than queens. Power could be passed from father to daughter, but the daughter's husband would be king. The Lady of Tikal became queen of Tikal in AD 511. We do not know her real name and she probably ruled alongside her husband. She was buried in a rich tomb, which shows that she was one of the most powerful Maya women.

Class structures

The king was the ultimate ruler in city-states, but the Maya also had clear ideas about social class beneath him. Family ties were important, and the most powerful families could trace their ancestors back over many generations. These noble families held most of the political and religious power in society. They included the scribes who were able to read and write Maya **hieroglyphs**, or picture writing. Many nobles lived and worked in the heart of the cities.

Free farmers were the ordinary people who owned some land to grow maize and other crops. This class was probably divided between wealthy and poorer farmers but they were better off than peasants, who worked on the land of the nobles or rich farmers, or as servants to the noble families.

Slavery

At the bottom of the pile were the **slaves**. Slaves could be criminals or prisoners captured in wartime. If children were born into slave families, they were slaves too. People could be bought out of slavery by wealthy relatives.

 CRIME AND PUNISHMENT

The Maya had a very strict law code. They believed that nothing happened by accident. If someone lost or damaged something belonging to another person they would have to pay for it. If they had no money to pay, they faced becoming a slave. The punishment for murder was execution, which could be carried out by the family of the victim. The Maya didn't put criminals in prisons; slavery was the punishment for crimes such as stealing.

Compare the fine clothes of the king and nobles at the top of Maya society to those of the working people at the bottom.

Religion affected all areas of Maya life. Kings were believed to be a link between the people and the gods, and priests were some of the most powerful people. The Maya name for a priest means "He of the Days" and it was a priest's job to mark time using the Maya calendar, as well as to perform the religious rituals that were a regular part of Maya life.

The Maya believed that time passed in cycles of just over 5,125 years. It has been claimed that the Maya expected the world to end and be reborn at the end of this Long Count, but we can't be sure about this. There were also many myths about how the world had been created, including the story of the Hero Twins, heroic sons of the Maize God.

The Temple of the Inscriptions at Palenque shows the importance of religion and ritual for the Maya.

ALL kinds of gods

The Maya believed in the existence of more than 100 different gods. Each god could also have many different forms: old or young, male or female, human or animal, or a combination of the two. New gods were often added and, over hundreds of years, some became less important.

Chahk is the god of rain, thunder and lightning. An able warrior, he is shown here holding an axe.

 MAYA GODS AND GODDESSES

Some of the most important Maya gods and goddesses were:

Itzamna
God of writing, learning and the sciences and often seen as the supreme creator god

K'inich Ajaw
The sun god and possibly a different aspect of Itzamna

Chahk
The rain god.
Each class and profession also had its own gods associated with it.

This **carving** shows a king and queen dressed in fine clothes. The queen is using thorns to draw blood from her tongue as a sacrifice to the gods.

Blood and sacrifice

One of the most remarkable features of Maya religion was the belief in self-sacrifice. Kings and nobles shed their own blood by cutting their tongues or other parts of their bodies. This blood was seen as a religious offering and essential to keep the gods happy.

If rulers were captured in war, they would be ritually sacrificed to the gods by the Maya priests. Ordinary people might have been sacrificed as well, but today's experts believe this wasn't very common. Animals and birds were more likely to be killed to honour the gods.

Death and the Afterlife

For the Maya, death was always present, whether through disease, war or sacrifice. They believed that, after death, a person's spirit would descend into the nine layers of the **Underworld**. Ordinary people were often buried beneath the floors of their houses, while nobles and kings were buried in magnificent tombs. Most people were buried with some food or the tools they used in their work, but the biggest tombs contained much more. One ruler from Tikal was buried with nine servants, who had been sacrificed to accompany their master to the Afterlife.

HOW DO WE KNOW?

Much of our knowledge of Maya religion is based on images found in temples and four codices (books made from long strips of bark) that have survived. Spanish invaders in the 1500s destroyed most Maya books. They wanted to convert the Maya to Christianity and wipe out all traces of their religion.

Most of the Maya worked on the land, whether it was their own land or that of rich farms and nobles. During the Classic Period, the population of city-states boomed and every scrap of land was needed to grow food. Farmers probably worked in large teams to clear and **irrigate** land, grow and harvest crops. Crops included maize, beans, chilli peppers, cacao, avocado, and cotton, which was used to make clothes.

Maya farmers had to use new techniques to get the best from their land. On swampy land, they dug out canals and raised the level of fields to help them grow more crops. Water plants from the canals were spread across the raised fields to make them more fertile.

Fishing and hunting

In Maya communities near the coast, fish were caught using hook and line or nets. Inland, drugs were added to streams, making the sleepy fish easier to catch. Turkeys were farmed for their meat and deer were hunted in the areas of forest that remained. Maya farmers also kept bees for honey.

 ## TOOL TECHNOLOGY

The Maya managed the efficient and intensive clearing and farming of their lands during the Classic Period without metal tools or ploughs. Their main tools were stone axes and we still don't know how they were able to cut down huge rainforest trees using these basic tools.

Maya farmers worked together to make sure the people of their city had enough to eat.

Most Maya rulers employed groups of musicians and dancers like these.

City Workers

Most of the goods the Maya needed for daily life, such as clothes and pottery, were made by families themselves or by others within the community. Other items, such as sharp tools or fine pottery, would have been made by skilled craftspeople and sold at markets in the cities. Merchants traded essential goods like sea salt, for preserving food, and luxury goods such as **jade**.

The lavish lifestyles of the Maya rulers also provided jobs for many people. Noble families would have employed cooks, servants and palace entertainers. Craftspeople would also have made luxury goods, such as jade jewellery and fine clothes, for the city's richer citizens.

DID THE MAYA HAVE TOILETS?

Archaeologists think that the Maya understood how to create water pressure. Man-made water channels discovered in Palenque show that engineers created a system of plumbing that allowed them to build fountains and possibly even toilets.

Building the cities

Thousands of workers would have been needed to build the pyramids and palaces of the Maya cities. It's likely that most people in a city-state had to give up some of their time to help finish these monumental projects. Giant blocks of stone had to be quarried, transported and put together not only without cranes but also without wheeled vehicles and metal tools. Artists and stonemasons were also needed to create the pictures and carvings that decorated the buildings.

This tower at Chichén Itzá was built to watch the movements of the planet Venus.

Top jobs

The best jobs in Maya society went to the noble families and those closest to the king. Priests worked in the great temples. Officials and generals helped to govern the city-state and fight its regular wars.

 ### MAYA ASTRONOMERS

The *Dresden Codex*, one of the few surviving Maya books, includes tables that accurately chart the movements of the planets Venus and Mars and the dates of **solar eclipses**. The Maya believed that the movements of stars and planets affected their lives, so their priests worked hard to understand the night sky.

Keepers of the holy books

The leading scribe was a very important person. This "royal librarian" is often shown with a bundle of pens or paper tied to his forehead in Maya art. He was the leading official, teacher, **astronomer** and minister, who agreed royal marriages and alliances with other states.

This scribe wears the signs of his profession – brushes and a small bundle of bark paper – in his headdress.

Knowledge is power

Scribes, who could read and write the Maya hieroglyphs, had very high status. Some kings even chose to be shown with bundles of pens to show that they were trained as scribes.

Scribes could be men or women. As well as understanding how to create hieroglyphs, scribes had to be skilled artists or sculptors to write the hieroglyphs in bark books or carve them on to stone columns. Scribes would also have taught in schools to pass their valuable skills on to the children of noble families.

Maya houses were arranged so that large family groups lived together, their homes built around a central courtyard. Most Maya families lived a very simple life, based around the farming year that dominated most of their lives.

However, everyone would have been aware of the religious rituals that were such a vital part of Maya society. New Year was an important time for everyone, and there were rituals and ceremonies throughout the year for groups such as farmers, beekeepers and craftspeople.

This figure of the Maize God dates from about AD 715. It shows the importance of this staple food to the Maya.

What did the Maya eat?

Food for most families was based on maize. The day usually began with a type of maize porridge, flavoured with chilli peppers. Workers would carry a pot of water mixed with bread with them to the fields. Maize was also mixed with other ingredients and cooked to make **tamales**. Occasionally, people might have the chance to eat meat, usually mixed with vegetables in a stew. Maya homes usually had their own small gardens where they could grow fruit and vegetables. We know little about what rich families ate, although fish and meat would have been more important parts of their diet.

Cacao beans are the seeds of the cacao tree. They form in long pods, which grow on the tree's trunk and branches.

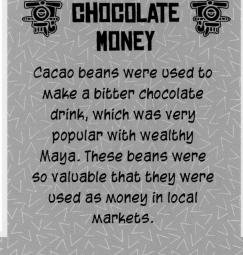

CHOCOLATE MONEY

Cacao beans were used to make a bitter chocolate drink, which was very popular with wealthy Maya. These beans were so valuable that they were used as money in local markets.

Maya marriages were carefully arranged to strengthen old family friendships or make new alliances.

Marriage

Family members usually arranged Maya marriages. Family ties were important and partners had to be chosen carefully – marriage to someone who had the same family name on their father's side was forbidden. Marriage created alliances between families, and these alliances meant a lot as families were expected to support each other in times of need.

 MAKING BABIES BEAUTIFUL

The Maya saw crossed eyes as a sign of beauty. Beads were hung over the noses of small children to try to make them cross-eyed. Noble Maya babies had their heads placed between two boards to give them the flat features that the Maya thought were most beautiful.

Growing up

As soon as a child was born, the parents would visit a priest to see what the future held for the new baby. Children had to grow up fast. In most ordinary families, children would be expected to help with household and farming chores as soon as they were able to. Only the children of the rich would receive an education. Most Maya never learned to read and write.

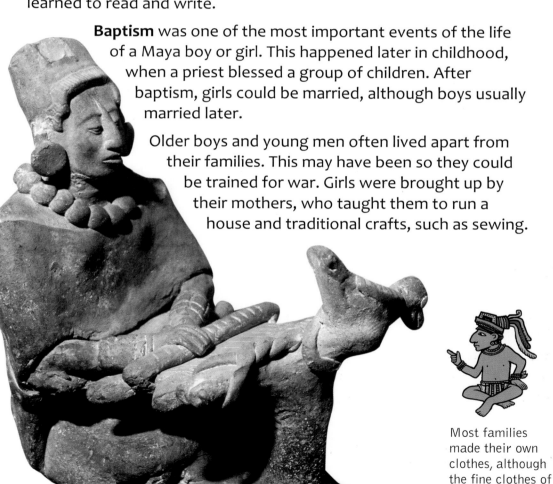

Baptism was one of the most important events of the life of a Maya boy or girl. This happened later in childhood, when a priest blessed a group of children. After baptism, girls could be married, although boys usually married later.

Older boys and young men often lived apart from their families. This may have been so they could be trained for war. Girls were brought up by their mothers, who taught them to run a house and traditional crafts, such as sewing.

Most families made their own clothes, although the fine clothes of the nobles would have been made by specialist craftspeople.

The way the Maya looked depended on their position in society. Ordinary people usually wore basic cotton clothes, such as a loincloth or simple cotton dresses. These clothes suited the hot climate and hard-working lives. At the top of the social scale, clothes were much more elaborate.

This vase painting shows how servants dressed in Maya palaces.

Noble men and women would wear brightly coloured clothes and would be adorned with the finest jewellery and accessories. For the Maya, that didn't mean gold and silver but jewellery made from precious green jade stone or oyster shells from the coast. The beautiful feathers of the quetzal bird were used to decorate their clothes and headdresses. Rulers had to have the finest and most extravagant clothes of all to show their power. Maya kings sometimes wore racks on their backs to support the giant headdresses they wore. Kings had long hair, covered with jewellery and ornaments.

Body decoration

Ordinary Maya made up for their simple clothes with body decorations. After they were married, both men's and women's upper bodies were covered with **tattoos**. Unmarried men and warriors painted their skin black. Teeth were filed into jagged patterns. The rich people inlaid tiny pieces of jade into their teeth.

This statue shows a noblewoman wearing jewellery and an elaborate headdress.

HOW DO WE KNOW?

Over hundreds of years, clothes rot away if they're not carefully preserved. What we know about Maya clothes is mostly based on modern Maya peoples, but also paintings and carvings. These mainly show the finery of kings and nobles, so we know more about them than about ordinary people.

For many years, archaeologists thought that the Maya were a peaceful people. Once they were able to read Maya hieroglyphs, it was clear that many of the carved stelae stones recorded war victories and defeats. By the end of the Classic Period, the city-states were at war with each other almost constantly.

Wall paintings from the small city of Bonampak show its people celebrating a victory, and the terrible fate of the losers.

Fire is Born

In AD 378, a stranger arrived in the Maya city of Waka. He came from the great city of Teotihuacan in central Mexico, and his name was Fire is Born. Within a few days he'd led his own troops and Waka's soldiers in an attack on the mighty city of Tikal. Fire is Born won and installed a new king, possibly an outsider from Teotihuacan. This was the start of the most warlike period in Maya history.

Different city-states gained or lost power over the centuries. The states of Tikal and Calakmul were bitter rivals during the Classic Period. They built alliances with smaller city-states to try to gain the upper hand. However, no state ever managed to control the whole Maya civilization during this time.

Success in war was a way for kings to win glory. The most successful, such as King Pacal of Palenque, were honoured as gods. However, the risks of waging war were great. Kings could be killed in battle. If they were captured, a worse fate awaited them – torture and sacrifice.

This stela from Tikal shows Fire is Born. He expanded the city's influence through wars and alliances.

The fighting season

Wars didn't last long. Rival city-states were often only separated by a day's march. It was important that the fighting season didn't clash with the time for planting and harvesting of crops, otherwise both sides could face starvation.

STINGING SURPRISE

Surprising the enemy was the key to victory. Some armies used unusual weapons such as fire or even hornets' nests thrown into enemy ranks to cause panic.

This vase painting shows a noble warrior preparing for battle.

MAYAPAN AND CHICHÉN ITZÁ

In the centuries before the Spanish invasion, the centre of Maya civilization shifted north to Chichén Itzá and Mayapan. The people of Chichén Itzá founded Mayapan in the 1200s, but the two cities later became enemies. In 1283, the ruler of Mayapan used battle-hardened **mercenaries** to capture Chichén Itzá, forcing its rulers into exile. They had to wait more than 150 years to get their revenge, encouraging nobles in Mayapan to revolt against their rulers, then destroying the city itself.

Into battle

The leaders of Maya armies were usually friends or relatives of the king. They dressed for battle with jade jewellery and quetzal feathers to show their importance.
Foot soldiers fought with war clubs tipped with razor-sharp blades of a rock called obsidian and spear-throwers that fired darts.

Battles often began with a surprise attack, and the capture of prisoners. **Pitched battles** between armies were fierce, bloody and noisy. A barrage of sound from drums, whistles and conch shells added to the din of the fighting itself.

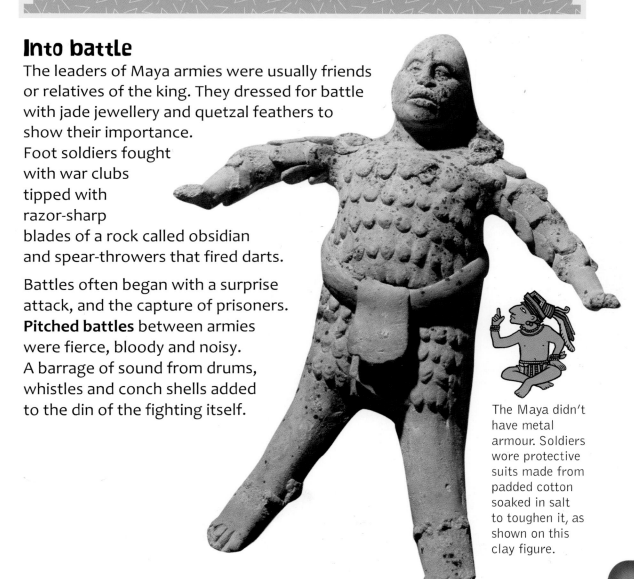

The Maya didn't have metal armour. Soldiers wore protective suits made from padded cotton soaked in salt to toughen it, as shown on this clay figure.

Religion was present in every aspect of Maya life, even their games. The Maya ball game, pok-a-tok, was more than just a sport. Winning or losing could mean the difference between life and death.

To win the game, players needed strength, stamina and good ball control.

The ball game

Ball courts shaped like a capital "I" have been found in the middle of many cities. Teams played pok-a-tok using a heavy rubber ball, which they had to move around the court without using their hands. The aim of the game was probably to get the ball through stone rings set into the sides of the court. There were spaces for spectators and the penalty for the losers was sometimes death. It was probably used as a way of settling disputes.

Music and dancing

It was probably only the noble families who really had time to relax. We know that royal households employed musicians. Wall paintings show musicians and dancers performing at celebrations and religious ceremonies. The Maya had many different dances, sometimes imitating the movements of animals such as the jaguar. It is likely that ordinary Maya made their own musical instruments from natural materials, including wood and shells.

HOW DO WE KNOW?

Archaeologists try to get as close to Maya life as they can. They study paintings and carvings and build versions of the trumpets or drums that the Maya played. They can even study the positions of dancers in the pictures to try to reconstruct their dances. Even so, they can never be sure if they have truly captured the music and movement of the Maya.

The Classic Period of Maya civilization prospered for hundreds of years from AD 250. However, after AD 800, some city-states stopped erecting the stelae that marked the reigns of their kings. The last stela in the great lowland city-states was erected in AD 909. In little more than a century, these thriving cities were abandoned. What happened to the Maya in this great collapse?

Intensive farming of the Maya lands would have made the soil less fertile, and more vulnerable to drought.

HOW DO WE KNOW?

Scientists have studied sediment from the bottom of a lake to determine what the climate was like at the time of the Maya collapse. By studying mud and shells from that time, they were able to discover that there was less rain in this period than at any other time for 7,000 years.

Experts have suggested several explanations. Early theories included the idea that the Maya were wiped out by a natural disaster, such as an earthquake or volcanic eruption. However, the Maya collapse didn't occur overnight but over several decades.

Military collapse

The city-state wars became more common and fiercer during the later Classic Period. Is it possible that the Maya simply destroyed themselves through conflict? The latest research shows that some city-states met a violent end, but this could have been caused by catastrophic **climate change** in the region.

Environmental change

The Maya depended on the annual harvest and they needed all available farmland to feed the growing population. A small change in climate could destroy the delicate balance of this system. Experts now believe that the Maya suffered from a series of devastating droughts.

The fate of the Maya

Failing harvests would have led to disastrous famines affecting millions. In turn, this probably made the wars more intense, as rulers tried to seize land to help feed their people. Ordinary Maya may have rebelled against the kings and nobles who lived in luxury while they starved. Failing harvests would have been seen as a sure sign that their kings had angered the gods.

INVASION!

Hernandez de Cordoba was the first Spanish explorer to visit the Maya lands in 1517. Maya warriors killed him, but a few years later more Spanish invaders arrived to conquer the region. The Maya fought back, using their knowledge of the land to evade the Spanish and launch surprise attacks. But by the end of the 1500s, the Spanish had conquered the resistance and went on to rule the region until about 1820.

After the Classic Period

The end of the Classic Period was disastrous, but it wasn't the end of the Maya. Northern cities, such as Chichén Itzá and Mayapan, continued to flourish, and their people may have included many who fled from the famine and disaster to the south.

Many Maya still live in traditional homes that are similar to the homes of their ancestors more than 2,000 years ago.

The Spanish invaders of the 1500s finally destroyed the Maya civilization. They brought with them diseases that wiped out many Maya communities. There are still around 8 million Maya in the world today. Many now share the culture of Mexico and other countries where they live, but there are still a few hundred Lakandon Maya who live a traditional way of life and follow some parts of the Maya religion.

A day in the life of a Maya boy

My name is Ah Maxam and I'm 12 years old. You could say I've had an easy life as my father, Lord Flint-face, and mother, Lady Water Venus, are rulers of the city-state of Naranjo. I'm training to be a scribe and artist, which isn't easy.

When I wake up, my servants look after my every need. They bring me my clothes and sandals. If it's a special day I'm expected to wear a fancy headdress with bright green feathers from the quetzal bird, but mostly I just wear the simple skirt of a scribe. Breakfast is maize porridge with some fruit.

Most of my day is spent with the other boys who are learning how to paint and carve hieroglyphs. We also learn maths and astronomy. Most of us come from rich families and our parents expect us to take over the running of the city. Our teacher is a very old and important scribe, and he gets annoyed when we get things wrong.

Sometimes I wonder why our system of writing has to be so complicated. If it was too easy, even peasants would understand it, and we probably wouldn't be in charge any more.

There is often some kind of religious ceremony, which isn't good if you don't like the sight of blood! Some of our gods are very special to scribes, such as One Monkey.

Being a scribe may sound a lot better than working in the fields but it can be dangerous. If there's a war, scribes are often first to be captured. Enemy scribes can get their fingers broken or their fingernails torn out – and that's if they're lucky!

TIMELINE

AROUND 800 BC
First villages are built in the lowland region of the Maya civilization

AROUND 300 BC
Building of El Mirador, one of the first great Maya cities

AROUND 100 BC
The great city of Teotihuacan is founded to the north of the Maya region

AROUND 250 AD
Beginning of the Classic Period of Maya civilization, with stelae being erected to mark the rule of kings in city-states

378 AD
Fire is Born defeats Tikal and takes over as its ruler

AROUND 500 AD
Tikal becomes the most powerful city in Maya civilization

511 AD
Lady of Tikal becomes ruler of the city-state as a child. She later rules alongside her husband.

595 AD
A volcanic eruption buries the village of Ceren. When it is discovered in 1978, it gives an important glimpse into the ordinary life of the Maya.

615 AD
Pacal becomes king of Palenque, which he rules for 68 years

AROUND 800 AD
Murals painted at Bonampak show the warlike nature of this city-state

869 CE
Construction ends at Tikal, marking the beginning of its decline

AROUND 900 CE
Most Maya cities in the lowland region are abandoned, although cities to the north are still flourishing

909 CE
The last stela is erected in the lowland region

1441
The city of Mayapan is defeated by the former ruling dynasty of Chichén Itzá

1517
Hernandez de Cordoba is the first Spanish explorer to visit Maya lands

1528
Spanish invasion of Maya lands begins

1566
Spanish Bishop Diego de Landa writes the first outsider's account of Maya civilization

1839
First expedition of American John Lloyd Stephens and British artist Frederick Catherwood to study the remains of Maya civilization

1952
Mexican archaeologist Alberto Ruz finds and excavates the tomb of King Pacal at Palenque

alliance partnership between two families or countries, to support each other

archaeologist person who studies the bones, tools and other objects of ancient people in order to learn about past human life and activities

astronomer scientist who studies space, stars and planets

baptism religious ceremony, usually welcoming a child into a religion

cenote natural well formed in limestone caves, or sinkhole

climate change changes in normal weather conditions for a region

hieroglyph picture symbol, as used in ancient Maya writing

irrigate use canals (or ditches) to carry water from a river or lake to crops in fields

jade precious hard stone, usually green, used for making jewellery and ornaments

lintel piece of wood across the top of a doorway

mercenary professional soldier hired to serve in a foreign army, usually for lots of money

pitched battle battle where both sides choose when and where they will fight

reservoir large, usually man-made lake used to collect water for use in a community

sacrifice killing of an animal or person as a religious offering to a god

slave someone who is forced to work without being paid

solar eclipse occasional event in which the Sun appears to be covered by the Moon

stela (plural: stelae) carved stone column that was marked with significant events from Maya history

tamale food made of maize dough, often mixed with meat or vegetables, and steamed

tattoo design on the skin made by puncturing it and adding coloured material

thatched roof on a building made of layers of dry vegetation such as straw or reeds

Underworld place where the Maya believed the spirits of the dead went

Books

Aztec, Inca and Maya (Eyewitness), Elizabeth Baquedano and Michel Zabe (Dorling Kindersley, 2011)

Lost Cities (Treasure Hunters), Nicola Barber (Raintree, 2013)

Mayan Civilization (The History Detective Investigates), Clare Hibbert (Wayland, 2014)

The Maya (Great Civilizations), Tracey Kelly (Franklin Watts, 2014)

Websites

www.britishmuseum.org/explore/cultures/the_americas/maya.aspx
Discover more about Maya treasures on this website.

www.history.com/topics/maya
This History Channel website includes articles and video clips about the Maya.

www.pbs.org/wgbh/nova/maya/
This site includes a video tour of the Maya ruins at Copan.

Places to visit

There are hundreds of large and small Maya sites in Central America. The most famous and important sites to visit are Palenque, Uxmal, Tikal, Chichén Itzá and Copan. You don't have to go all the way to Central America to see the treasures of the Maya civilization though, you can see some in museums here in the UK.

British Museum
Great Russell Street
London
WC1B 3DG

www.britishmuseum.org

INDEX